Preface

With rise in broadband network and wi-fi, more and more applications are moving to server side. Client side has very little footprint. This allows more control of the application in developer hands and they can release software without forcing client to update. This also brings up a new challenge where same server side is app is now shared among all users of the application. It is critical that as number of users grow, application continue to perform reasonably well. Scalability measurement is all about application's capability to withstand large number of users without degradation in performance.

This book offers a unique perspective on scalability. It talks at great length about why scalability is important. It also talks about how to tackle scalability measurements using key performance indicators. It illustrated step by step load test measurements using Visual Studio Team System which is on of the most popular tool among software engineers.

This book in intended for software engineers, engineering managers and product managers who are passionate about scalability. Scalability must never be an afterthought. It has to be incorporated in the application right from design stage. Also scalability measurements need to happen every time before releasing the product. It should be part of quality gate in CI-CD environment, This would allow engineers to catch performance bug before they reach customer.

About Authors

Ravindra Sadaphule

Ravindra Sadaphule is software professional with 20 years of programming experience. He works in Silicon Valley. He is passionate about solving problems and writing reusable, extensible and maintainable code. He has built several SaaS applications for web, iOS and android platforms. He has done MBA (IT management) from American Public University , USA and Bachelor of Engineering from Mumbai University. He can be reached at rsadaphule@gmail.com. He has also written book on Creational Design patterns in Java.

Sagar Deshpande

Sagar Deshpande completed engineering in Electronics in 2005 from a small town – Chandrapur in India. From school time itself, his dream was to tag himself as a "Software Engineer". His career started as a software developer with Microsoft technology. A complete career shift happened and landed him into an automation testing then converted to scalability testing stream. He started enjoying this new stream and observed it to be more interesting looking from the perspective of scalability tester. Scalability testing is completely different than normal testing and he is thankful to his career start to have a perspective of developer that helps digging more into the root cause analysis for any performance test issue. He is doing scalability testing from last 8+ years now that include code profiling and load testing for standalone and hosted applications. He is writing this book to present his perspective of what a scalability testing is, his thought process, why he feels it is different and how he has developed this perspective. He can be reached at deshpande.sagar.s@gmail.com .

Chapter 1
Perspective

"You've got to start with the customer experience and work backwards to the technology." – Steve Jobs

Usually when software projects are delivered under right deadlines, engineer mostly focus on functional testing and forget about scalability testing. Also I have seen that scalability testing is usually performed towards the end of project. The problems identified in final stages are usually patched (band-aid) and not a good long term solutions. These practices usually come back to bite us during maintenance use. This results in customers experiencing latency issues and logging numerous complaints and thus it erodes customers trust in the application. It costs time and money to the company. Such services can't be considered as assets to the company. Regardless of amount of hard work put in by developers, it build mistrust about them in senior leadership's minds.

The most important aspects of service users is that they don't need to loyal to the service as they have not invested any money in it. There is high completion for some online services like e-commerce. A poorly performing site could cause user to move away to competitors service and never come back.

Forrester Research conducted in 2006 to test performance maturity of organizations and its impact on defect rate. The companies who did little or no performance testing had to resolve 100% of their defects after releasing code to their customers. The companies which did performance testing late in the software development lifecycle, defect rate in production was 30%. For companies who did performance testing right from the beginning phase, defect rate was merely 5%. This data is summarized in table below.

Approach	% of Defects Resolved in production
firefighting	100%
Performance Validation	30%
Performance Driven	5%

Needless to say, scalability testing should not be after thought. It has to be done in incremental and iterative fashion during the project development.

Before performance testing is performed, one needs to understand how current service is being used by users. The service usually offers multiple feature and each of these features has different user engagement. In addition, one also need to understand what are peak periods for the service. For instance e-commerce sites like amazon.com, walmart.com have very high traffic on Black friday. Understanding those peak patterns will help get an idea of maximum load that service need to withstand and also amount of time for which it needs to withstand peak load. I am providing a general guidelines on what questions engineer should be asking product manager below. This will help engineer to configure and perform realistic load testing

- ✓ How many users will use the the application concurrently?
- ✓ What are peak period days and what is maximum user traffic?
- ✓ Does the traffic vary per feature in the application?
- ✓ What are most heavily used features in the application?
- ✓ Where are our users located?

Engineer should also establish right metrics for measuring scalability characteristics of the system. These metrics are known as KPI (Key performance Indicators). These metrics are defined below.

- **Latency:** Latency describes response time that user sees after initiating request. In a typical web application we usually measure 99th percentile latency. 99th percentile latency describes worst case latency as observed by 1% of users. For example if 99th percentile latency is 250 ms and you have 100 users, it means 99 out of 100 users see latency less than 250 ms. The latency is usually measured at peak load

- **Availability:** Availability measures success rate of the application. It's percentage ratio of successful requests vs total requests in a given day. For instance, if your application receives 50,000 requests per day and out to that 45,000 requests are successful, then availability of application is 45,000*100/50,000 = 90%

- **Throughput:** Throughput measures number of requests your application can press per unit of of time. So if your application can process 300 requests in one second, then throughput is 300 requests per second.

- **Memory Utilization:** Memory utilization describes percentage amount of total memory that the service is using. For instance if s server has 12 GB of RAM and the service is 8 GB , then memory utilization is 66.67%. Usually it's advisable to keep memory utilization under 75% under peak load to account for additional spikes.

- **CPU Utilization:** CPU utilization describes percentage amount of total CPU time that the service is using.. Usually it's advisable to keep CPU utilization under 75% under peak load to account for additional spikes.

To ensure great success, performance testing must be taken into considered right from requirements phase. Agile development dictates software development in incremental and iterative manner. At the end of each iteration, performance testing must be conducted and KPIs must be evaluated. Doing it each iteration will help find bugs quickly as code churn between two successive iteration is small . This will also set goo rhythm and discipline among developers to tackle performance issues long before customer sees it.

Chapter 2
Scalability Vs Performance

In 1980s, Tim Berners Lee, a British Scientist demonstrated working model of protocols linking hypertext documents and that marked beginning of modern internet. Several applications like email, instant messenger, online shopping revolutionized lives of people. Demand for increasing amounts of data exchange over internet gave rise to broadband networks. Most of the desktop application were moved to web as it offered low client footprint, platform independence for consumers and ability to roll out updates frequently. This however also presented a new challenge. In desktop applications, usually the application is entirely used by one user. Most of the processing on client machine. Every client had their own application. As long as the could process **one** user's request in reasonable time, it was considered ok. From testing perspective all we needed to is to measure time taken for an operation for a single user. This testing is called performance testing,

    As these apps moved to internet, the app infrastructure on server is now shared among all users. All users use same app using a thin client like browser. Since server infrastructure have limited resources like machines, CPU, memory, We also needed a way to ensure as number of users increase, resources are used in optimal way and overall performance for average user is not impacted. Scalability measures ability of server to withstand **large** number of users without significant impact on latency. Performance testing measures latency for single user request while scalability ensures that latency does not get significant impact as number of users grows. An average response time of 2 second is considered acceptable. If your service takes more than 2 seconds tp respond to user's request, user is most likely to go away and use some other application. This is not a healthy sign.

    This can be achieved using distributed and stateless system design of the service. You can think of service world and a freeway with multiple lanes say 4, and cars in the lane can be thought is as users. One slow car in any one lane could slow down all the cars behind it. All it takes is 4 slow cars, one in each lane to bring entire freeway to standstill. Similarly few users for a service could bring down entire service, if their requests are not handled in reasonable time. Therefore it is of paramount importance test for scalability before releasing service. Scalability testing is done using load testing where we generate increasing synthetic user load in steps and observe vital statistics like 99th percentile latency, CPU utilization, memory utilization, disk utilization. We then try to analyze performance bottleneck in the code under code and attempt to solve it. We could solve the problem by fixing the code or using additional machines. There are several tools like VSTS, Jmeter or roadrunner available in the market that can help you with performance testing. Here is a gray that shows typical load testing results. It shows latency (Y-axis) Vs number of concurrent users (X-azis)

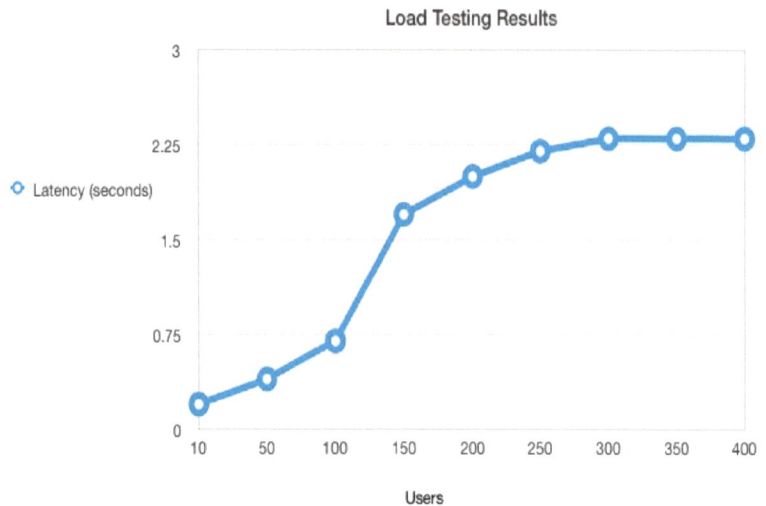

Scalability testing is also useful for future capacity planning. When your product manager tells you that releasing a new feature would expect to grow user traffic by 2X in next 3 months, then you may need to test if current infrastructure can withstand the load or you would need to add more servers to handle the increased load.

You might hear terms like stress testing and soak testing. These are variants of load testing. The purpose of stress testing is to increase the load on the service until service crashes so that we can find maximum number of users that we can server. The purpose of soak testing is to run load testing for extended period of time to ensure that service can withstand large load for extended periods.

Chapter 3
Load Testing Objectives

Objectives of Load Testing differs with each product and its architecture and technology. However, below objectives will guide you to decide on the reasons to perform Load testing on a given project.

Why Objectives are important

It is very important that Load Testing objectives are defined clearly at the beginning itself before starting the project. Once you understand the application, you should be able to draw your needs and requirements to define Load testing objectives. The objectives should answer "**Why**" part of Application's Load testing needs. You should be convinced with "Why" part before proceeding with actual work.

With clear objectives, vision would be clear and hence activities around load testing can be defined and planned accordingly. Lot of time it is seen that people just take load test executions without even knowing if the result would really of any help to conclude with the available data/information. When objectives are not clear, there is no direction to the work that gets performed and hence conclusions won't be valid.

Objectives should address all the Load testing requirements of application under test. If you miss to define any objective, it can lead to a gap which can have ripple effect on overall application load and scalability plan which in-turn affect Organization with its reputation.

How to define Load testing objectives

To define objectives, it is required that detailed application understanding is taken. Along with application workflows, it is important to understand;

- Application Architecture
- Application deployment Architecture (infrastructure)
- Load testing needs

To get clarity on these details, you would need to come up with detailed needs document or questionnaire to keep as a checklist that needs to be answered by Stakeholders.

It is always better to prepare a set of questionnaire to get these questions answered from stakeholders.

Few examples are;

- Understand overall load testing need
    - What problem is trying to be solved?
    - What are the known pain points and limitations today?
- Application Overview

- o Understand purpose of application
- o Discuss most important end to end business scenarios.
- o Identify the major application functionalities
- o Walkthrough Architecture.
- o Scheduled job details

- User Profile
  - o Define user personas
  - o Collect user metrics

- load Testing Goals and Objectives
  - o Establish expectations from application owner
  - o Review test strategy and plan

- Data Generation Needs
  - o Identify test data requirements
  - o Review any tools already in existence that will generate data

- Test Environment
  - o Determine what will be used for a test environment
  - o How will it differ from production?

Examples - Load Testing Objectives

Demystifying Scalability

- Product understanding

    o Understand product from end users perspective to establish comprehensive load testing process

    o Product understanding from end users perspective

    o Understand application and deployment architecture

- Identifying critical business scenarios

    o Depending on usage pattern of an application, identify most used scenarios

    o Scenarios can either be developed from production usage pattern (for live applications) or from BAs (for new applications)

- Identify "Real" user load capacity of an application

    o Real users are anticipated simulated user load for an application at peak

- Identify load bottlenecks
- Identify Web and DB server capacity
    - With single and multi-server setup
- Identify services throughput
    - For service/API based application, identifying throughput of each service is required
    - Identify minimal hardware requirement needed for supporting expected user load
    - Helps in Modeling out hardware requirements for anticipated user load
- Identify how many Web instances can be supported by shared database instance
- Identify Optimization areas
    - With DB configuration testing and VM configuration testing
- Identify application limiting factors
    - App/Web servers?
    - DB Server?
    - Network/Bandwidth?
    - Storage?

Chapter 4

Load Testing Approach

Once the objectives are defined, load testing approach needs to be planned and prepared. It starts with identifying load testing pre-requisite.

Identifying Load Test Pre-requisite

This step is the most critical step in the overall process. You need to foresee all the requirements and needs to execute your project smoothly. You cannot go to your stakeholders now and then just to get pre-requisite data that should be blocking you each time to proceed further. Nobody would entertain you if this steps are not predefined and clearly communicated in the starting phase. Below topics needs to be kept in mind while identifying pre-requisite for any application under load test;

Identify Data Generation requirements

Data is the heart of application. Application cannot run without data. Each transaction either create or manipulate data in its own sense. Behavior of application is purely data dependent. The internal code behaves or responds differently with the changing volume of data/information it has to process. Keeping these dependencies on application data in mind it's always recommended to carry out load testing on pre-populated dataset rather than testing on a fresh or blank one. Problem with fresh data set is that, you won't be able to find out data induced problem, only load induced problems can be identified. Production scrubbed DB is the best choice, however, if it is not available due to various reasons like legality, data size, geo locations etc; data generation should be planned by understanding application data integrity and complexity such that it matches close to production.

In addition to application data, test/input data is equally important. There are lot of parameter that needs to be considered while creating input data set like;

- User Types (Admin, Local, General)
- User Distribution
- User Mix (like, 80% new users, 20% returning users)
- User Roles and permissions
- Expected users at a given period of time (say one day or one week)
- Expected total number of users of the system
- Expected maximum number of logged-in users
- Expected total number of concurrent users
- Expected Peak user count

Finalize Test scenarios

Scenarios are the steps/activity that an end user is expected to perform on an application. To draft scenarios for load test, most used scenarios needs to be identified. Unlike automation testing, all scenarios cannot be covered in load testing.

For Live applications, scenarios can be created by analyzing its production usage pattern and information that can be captured by various monitoring tools or logs. For Web based applications, IIS Logs can be used to identify how application is being used. Similarly, DMVs (Dynamic Management Views) can also be used to track DB transactions to define usage.

For new applications where production data is not available, you need to rely on BAs and Stakeholders.

Not just scenarios, but its usage or frequency is also important to know. How user is actually executing a scenario in a specified time duration is what determines its frequency or throughput. This throughput can then be used to configure load test to simulate real user situations.

Throughput Calculations

For each identified scenario, its frequency or throughput is required to be calculated to simulate transactions for a given user load. Each user in real life may or may not just navigate only 1 scenario. Use activities also depends on the type of user. Users may also perform activities cross modules.

To simulate all such situations, throughput based model works best. Rather than simulating actual number of anticipated user load of an application under test, simulate user activities or transactions anticipated to be performed by those users which in-turn simulate anticipated usage and load on servers by those users.

Below example will explain you what information is required to design throughput based user pace approach and how to use this information to configure your load test executions.

Example

Scenario	(A) % user executing this scenario	(B) Number of times scenario being executed in an hour	Throughput for given "Real" user load				
			(C) 1000	2000	3000	4000	5000
Scenario-1	40%	3	1200	2400	3600	4800	6000
Scenario-2	30%	5	1500	3000	4500	6000	7500
Scenario-3	50%	2.5	1250	2500	3750	5000	6250
Scenario-4	20%	4	800	1600	2400	3200	4000

Above example explains details about how to calculate throughput to simulate different user load. The term "Real user" is nothing but a self-created term in this situation.

Explanation – Consider a situation where there are 4 scenarios identified from multiple modules. Column – A and Column – B should be provided by BAs or stakeholders or by analysing production usage. This is nothing but an anticipated behavior of given users for a particular scenario.

Here it is read as; 40% of 1000 users (Column – C) are expected to perform Scenario-1, 3 times in an hour. So the expected transaction rate or throughput of Scenario-1 for 1000 users would be 1200. Similarly, 50% of 1000 users are expected to perform Scenario-3, 2.5 times in an hour. Expected throughput for Scenario-3 for 1000 users would be 1250. Holistically, *if we achieve above throughput for all scenarios for a given user load and application performs as expected, we can say that application supports that given user load*. For other user load it is just a mathematical calculations.

Define SLA(s), KPIs/Acceptance criteria

Once the scenarios are identified, you would need their respective SLAs or KPIs. We need to define criteria's that will determine if an application can be said degraded with increasing user load.

KPI or SLA numbers are used to define these different criteria. These numbers are either provided by stakeholders depending on the complexity of a web page or any other calculation that may affect response time which is known and communicated to customers.

Considering all these multiple changing parameters, each scenario should different SLAs or KPIs defined along with their internal business transactions. You should also validate your load test numbers against these SLAs to

Demystifying Scalability

conclude on the status of application under test by which your objectives can be concluded.

Load Test Approach

The pre-requisite once defined, you would need to use that information and design your test approach. Test approach consists of different steps/processes that may or may not apply to each and every project as a whole. It totally depends on the tool which you plan to use, its limitations, application data structure and application technology stack.

I am providing here example of basic web application testing approach that can be directly applicable to VSTS based load testing;

Tool Selection

Depending on the application technology stack and compatibility, tool can be selected from various tools available in the market. Keep all your load test objectives in mind before selecting on a tool.

Other parameter that may impact your decision on tool selection is its license cost. It is advisable to use licensed version on load testing tool so that complete information can be extracted. Trail or evaluation version may work well to simulate user load, however, if you can't get raw data out of it, it would be useless as for deeper analysis you may require complete data. Analysis is a backbone of Load Testing so you would need to double check if all the information can be extracted out of the tool in the POC phase. Without analysis, the value of Load testing is zero.

Below is a list of tools that are commonly used for Load testing and its result analysis. There are many others as well, however, you need to choose them as required.

Name	Load Testing	Code Profiling	Open Source
VSTS 2013, 2015	•	•	
SQL Server 2012, 2014	•	•	
Idera - DB Analysis	•	•	
Fiddler	•	•	•
Jmeter (if required)	•		•
Load Runner (if required)	•		
New Relic - Service profiling	•	•	
RTMonitor (Run Time Monitor)	•		•
WCF Trace Unit - scripting	•		•
SQL Diag/Nexus - DB Analysis	•		•
Dead Lock Detector - DB Analysis		•	
RML Utility - DB Load testing	•		•
ANTS Profiler - Code Profiling	•	•	
WANem - Network Emulator		•	•
Snoop - WPF applications		•	•

Threshold Calculations

A new concept is introduced by us as Performance Violations. So far capacity is determined directly by checking if the SLAs are met or when actual error occurs or application starts to break. However, it is also important to check when your application starts to slow down on its responsiveness. Performance violation Rate help you determine this by defining a threshold value.

Performance violation is calculated based on Threshold value of a given scenario. It could be at scenario level or deeper at transaction level. It could be your own choice. Number of iterations that takes more time to complete than this defined threshold value, contributed towards Performance violation number.

Below example will guide you on how to define these values when SLA/KPIs are not available.

Example

Defining Threshold Value:

- Record Test time for complete scenario and their transactions under No load (Single user test)

- Threshold value = Recorded Time of No Load * 1.5

    o There is no industry standard. These values can be SLA values. In SLA case, no load test is not required.

- Assign thresholds at Scenario and Transaction level

Login Reduction

In almost all application now, authentication is strictly followed. More and more authentication mechanisms are floating around. Even with a normal authentication at service level, token needs to be passed to underlying services. This restrict users to perform scenario bypassing login which results in large number of login transactions as it will be executed with each iteration. One way to overcome this problem is to create end to end scenario, but that will introduce more complexity to maintain different throughput values. Another way that we have created is with the help of Plugin.

```
private void TestStartingUp(object source, ... TestStartingUpEventArgs)
{
    lock (this)
    {
        bool flag = false;
        testStartingUpEventArgs.TestContextProperties.Add("ScenarioName", testStartingUpEventArgs.ScenarioName);
        // code continues...
        for (int i = 0; i < GenericScenarioName.List.Count; i++)
        {
            if (GenericScenarioName.List.ContainsKey(testStartingUpEventArgs.ScenarioName))
            {
                testStartingUpEventArgs.TestContextProperties.Add("TokenShareFlag", GenericScenarioName.List[testStartingUpEventArgs.ScenarioName].TokenShareFlag);
                if (GenericScenarioName.List[testStartingUpEventArgs.ScenarioName].ScenarioName == scenarioName.Complete(testStartingUpEventArgs.UserContext.UserId) &&
                    GenericScenarioName.List[testStartingUpEventArgs.ScenarioName].ScenarioUserCount.TestStartingUpEventArgs.UserContext.UserId] != 0)
                {
                    if (GenericScenarioName.List[testStartingUpEventArgs.ScenarioName].ScenarioUserCount[testStartingUpEventArgs.UserContext.UserId] >
                        GenericScenarioName.List[testStartingUpEventArgs.ScenarioName].ScenarioUserCountMax[testStartingUpEventArgs.UserContext.UserId])
                    {
                        flag = true;
                        GenericScenarioName.List[testStartingUpEventArgs.ScenarioName].ScenarioUserCount[testStartingUpEventArgs.UserContext.UserId] = 0;
                    }
                    GenericScenarioName.List[testStartingUpEventArgs.ScenarioName].ScenarioUserCount[testStartingUpEventArgs.UserContext.UserId] += 1;
                }
                else
                {
                    GenericScenarioName.List[testStartingUpEventArgs.ScenarioName].ScenarioUserCount.Remove(testStartingUpEventArgs.UserContext.UserId);
                    GenericScenarioName.List[testStartingUpEventArgs.ScenarioName].ScenarioUserCount.Add(testStartingUpEventArgs.UserContext.UserId, 1);
                    flag = true;
                }
                testStartingUpEventArgs.TestContextProperties.Add("Iteration", GenericScenarioName.List[testStartingUpEventArgs.ScenarioName].ScenarioUserCount[testStartingUpEventArgs.UserContext.UserId]);
            }
            break;
        }
    }
}
```

Above code snippet is an example of a scenario in a plugin. Similar code can be added or parameterized for rest of the scenarios. You need to specify number of iterations you want to execute with each login and this code will then takes care of bypassing the login for those many virtual users. You would need to make sure to write a code to save token that needs to be passed to next iterations. Multiple implementation options available with you are;

- A token is **saved and passed** to next login
- Logout after specified **iteration** completes
- Logout only after specified **time** is over

User Based Approach

Considering lot of limitations with other Load test mix provided by VSTS, I found User Pace approach most promising and fits to almost all application that are under test.

As we already know the throughput that needs to be achieved for each scenario under test, we can configure load test with the use of these throughput numbers. Before proceeding with the implementation of user based approach, you would need to determine Average Response Time of the scenario with very low (even 1) user load. This is required to determine maximum number of iterations that can be executed in an hour.

For e.g. if Scenario-1 takes on an average 60 secs to complete its execution for 2 users, it means throughput (per user per hour) cannot be greater than 60 (60/3600). If it is 90, then throughput cannot be greater than 45 (90/3600). However, we must consider to put additional pacing between two iterations as we know that under load application load start to degrade. This will make sure that expected throughput is achieved for that scenario even if few iterations takes longer than usual time to complete their execution.

Below load test configuration are required to create load test file;

Scenario	User Load (to achieve 1000 real user throughput)	Throughput
Scenario-1	40	30
Scenario-2	50	30
Scenario-3	25	50
Scenario-4	20	40

For increasing/decreasing users, only User load would be changed keeping throughput constant. As there is no point of increasing throughput for the same reason mentioned above.

With this approach, advantages are, taken any slice for any given time, there will always a concurrency achieved for each and every scenario under test.

Demystifying Scalability

Below is a screenshot of detailed test section of VSTS about how it executes throughout the test period;

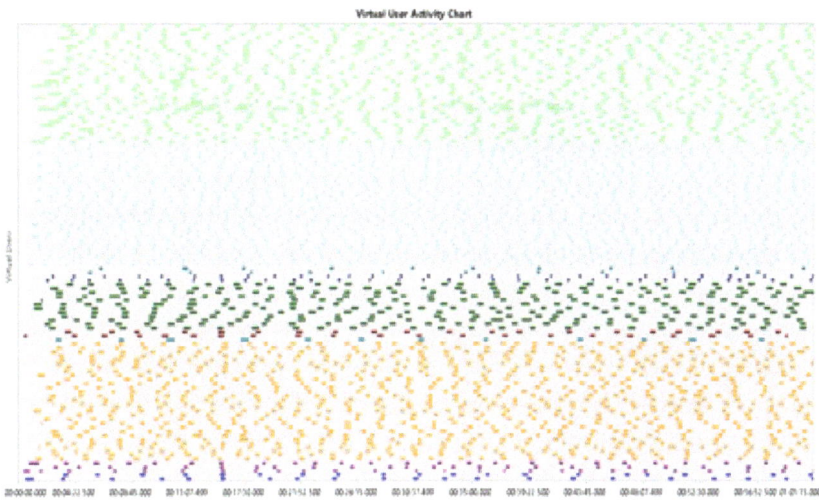

For detailed understanding of different test mix models of VSTS please refer - VSTS Test Mix Models in Detail

Application Capacity and Breaking Point

The usual behavior of application under load is that; on a given infrastructure, with increasing user load load of an application observed to be stable till certain point (Capacity point) after which load/responsiveness of an application starts to degrade. With further increase in user load, a "Breaking Point" can be observed at which all the resources of the servers are seen saturated resulting in exponential rise in response time of almost all scenarios and breaking the system completely.

Demystifying Scalability

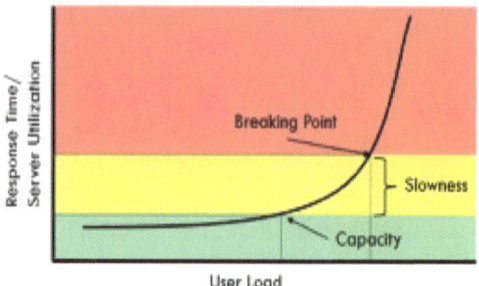

This particular behavior can be simulated with Step user load approach where a user load is gradually increased by tweaking the load test setting of "Step Duration", "Step User Count", "Initial User count" and "Ramp up Rate" and kept at that load for specified fixed duration.

Load Test Execution

Load test is executed after scripting the scenarios. There are lot of ways a load test can be executed. Either in a mix of scenarios or individually for each scenario. It is recommended to execute it in a mix as it shows the overall behavior of an application under test. Below are few methodologies used in load test executions;

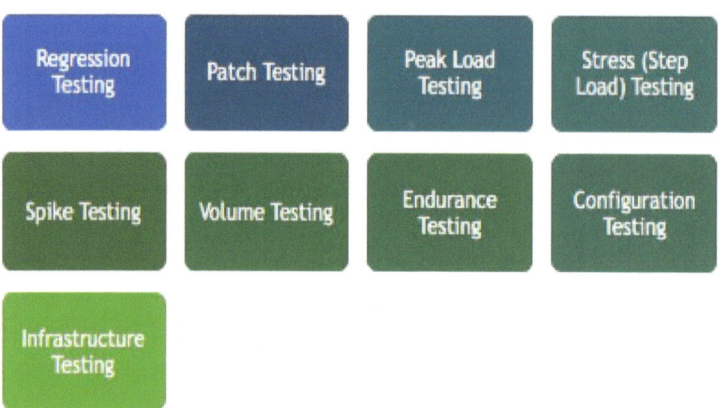

Regression Testing

Baselining is done to determine application behaviour at the capacity load. Baseline include all the information related to load test execution including performance counters for we/app servers and any server profiling data (if available).

Once the baseline is established, regression testing can be performed for changing builds/code. A frequency is required to be set for these changes that will decide on regression frequency.

The purpose of regression testing is to identify impact of the changes in the code/build on the Load and scalability of the application or area of an application under test. Regression testing ensures that there is a continuous test cycles for technology releases which also make sure that issues are identified early in the life cycle.

Patch Testing

Demystifying Scalability

Most of the time code change is required to be tested before it gets into the build. Apart from code changes, SP change, configuration change is also required to be tested. These tests to check the impact is termed as Patch testing.

These patches are received from development team, architects or DBAs in terms of a deployment items as a special fix or code change. These are tested and compared against baseline to identify whether it is showing an improvement or degradation.

A complete analysis is required to be done for the area patch is provided.

Patch testing is not necessarily a required step for any test cycle. It is required to be tested as needed.

Peak Load Testing

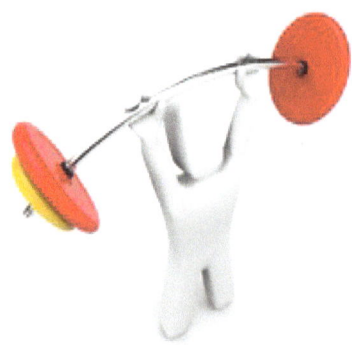

Peak Load testing is performed to determine if an application under test supports expected peak user load. The user load is simulated with respect to expected usage pattern of pre-defined scenarios.

Peak load test is carried out at a load between capacity and up to breaking point of an application.

This test is performed for each build or change to determine expectations are being met. It is also used to identify any modifications required to code, configuration or infrastructure to achieve expected load.

Stress (Step Load) Testing

Stress or Step load testing is performed to identify breaking point and Capacity point of an application.

User load is gradually increased in the form of steps. At each level, the load is maintained for definite time period and again a step of load is increased. Test identifies where maximum limits are of the application before breaking

Step load test helps in identifying infrastructure requirements for any anticipated user load. In addition to this, it also helps in determining or modelling out infrastructure changes required for seasonal applications.

Step load test is required to be performed for all major technology releases.

Configuration testing

Configuration testing is designed to test mainly multiple infrastructure and application configuration. As name suggest, any configuration changes at application or infrastructural level is tested and compared against baseline.

Configuration testing helps validate capacity and infrastructure change plan with future looking projections to confirm their readiness

Volume Testing

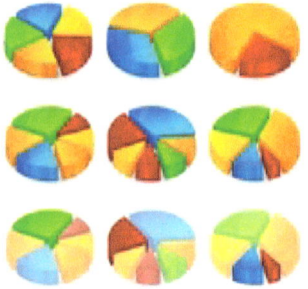

Volume testing is to identify behavior of application for changing data volume.

For a DB sensitive applications, application responsiveness depends a lot on its data volume. Such applications are required to be tested for multiple set of dataset that has anticipated and projected data growth.

Volume testing is mainly a future looking testing and it is very important that data growth is precisely projected.

Spike Testing

Spike testing is majorly done to determine application and infrastructure response to sudden burst of concurrent load on the system. This is an adhoc type of testing.

Understanding of changing usage pattern is required to plan Spike test. Spike test is more like a scenario creation that come once a while, however, it helps in planning infrastructure components that can handle the behavior of application during those situations.

Infrastructure Testing

Infrastructure testing is done to determine behavior of different infrastructure component like Storage, Memory, Network, Latency, etc.

Infrastructure testing is more a resiliency testing of an application on a defined infrastructure. In this test, failure scenarios as well as failover scenarios are tested.

It is becoming a norm now to plan this test for any application that is required to do Load testing.

Load Test Terminologies

Load test

Load test is used for performing load test on an application. It simulates multiple users as virtual users and executes the test scripts to simulate the real user load on different servers like Application Server, Database server and Web server. Load test can be used with any of the test scripts

Think Time

Think time is the time taken between two requests. This can be the time taken by the user to fill a form, view a page or reading some text etc. Think times are used for simulating the real user scenario; how the system will work with a real user

Constant Load

Constant load means same number of users hit the system from the starting of the test till the end. It is like 25 users are using the system for a period of 1hr. All 25 users are hitting the system continuously. This type of testing is mainly used for stress testing

Step Load

In step load, users will join in a step manner. This is the same as different users hitting the system in various times and the number of users in a system is not constant. Following parameter needs to be specified in step load pattern

Start User Count

How many users should hit the system at the time of test start

Step Duration

After how many seconds the next users should join the system

Step user Count

How many user needs to join the system after step duration

Maximum User Count

What is the Maximum users that you want to execute with

Test Mix

Test Mix specifies how different scenarios are executed or used in the system. Different test mixes are formed by studying the system's usage.

For example, if we are doing a load testing on online marketing site; around 60% people will search for different products, 30% will buy few products and 10% bookmark the products. From this usage information, we can form a test mix as 60% simulated users will execute the script for search, 30% will execute the script for buying a product and remaining 10% will execute the script for bookmarking a product

Baseline Test

Baseline is a test that needs to be taken to understand the behavior of application and resources at capacity. This test is used to compare against a repeated test that is carried out to test an impact of any change in code or change in a complete build.

Response Time

Most of the load test is done to understand the response time of an application in a given load. If an application is not completed its load test, then the response time for an expected user load may not be defined.

Response time is the time taken by a transaction to respond to the user. If the response time is very high, the user experience will be low and the usage of the application may affect it. For decreasing the response time at the same time keeping the rich user interface is one of the challenges.

Throughput

Throughput is the number transactions or inputs handled by the server per second. This indicates how much load or requests the server can handle at once. Depends on the throughput and response time requirements we may plan the clustering of servers

Resource Utilization

Resource utilization includes the servers' processor, memory and network utilizations. How much the application utilizing the server resources determine, whether we can go with a single server or need to have multiple servers or not.

These are three major terms or measures we use in load test. Apart from these measures, we have network time, latency time, request time, test mix, load mix, etc

Performance Counters

Performance counters are resource utilization information of web/app/DB server which can be captured using multiple tools along with a windows provided tool called "Perfmon". You have to setup different counter set depending on the application type you are testing.

Baseline Test

Baseline is a test that needs to be taken to understand the behavior of application and resources at capacity. This test is used to compare against a repeated test that is carried out to test an impact of any change in code or change in a complete build.

Chapter 5
Load Testing in Action

Load Test Architecture and Configuration

Load test rig

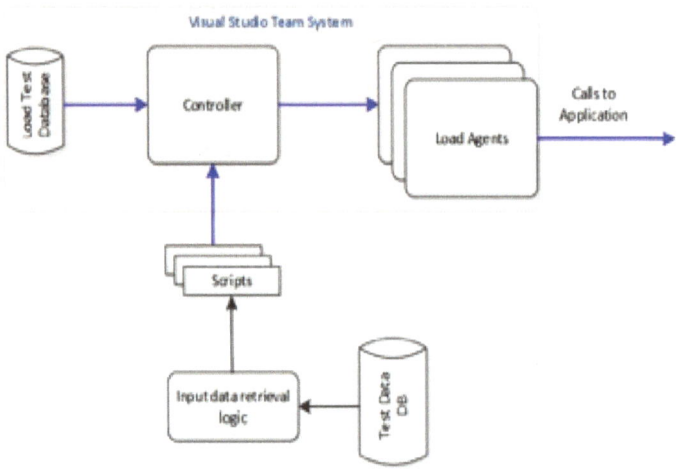

Load test rig is a combination of Controller with one or more Agents machines.

The Test controller manages test executions by communicating with Test Agents to start tests, stop tests, track test agent status, and collect test results. When all test agents are ready, the test controller sends a message to the test agents to start the test & distribute tests among all agents depending on the configured distribution.

Agent spins threads for each virtual user required for a test. Agents simulates virtual user activity and all tests are actually executed on Agents only. Each test agent runs the same load test.

The Controller & Agents could be physical or virtual machines. The controller is configured with the agents through Visual Studio to communicate with each other.

Visual Studio Team System (VSTS)

We will be using Visual Studio Team System (VSTS) to perform load testing. Its available with Visual Studio Professional or Ultimate edition. More information on licensing is available here.

Configuring Controller - Agents

Controller

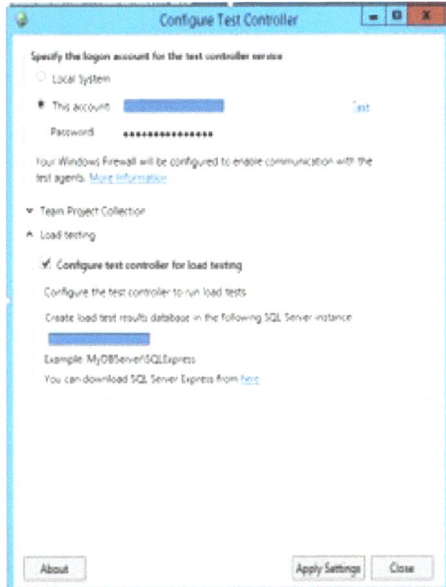

After installing Visual Studio Team Suite – Ultimate version, you have to install "Visual Studio Test Controller" on the controller machine (VM/Physical machine that is identified as controller) machine. Once the controller is installed, you need to open "Configure Test Controller", a screen as shown will open;

1. This Account – User on Controller machine with its domain. The same user needs to be created on Agent machine as well. It is advisable to add this user to Administrator group.

2. Password – Password for given user to authenticate. The username and password for Agents should also be same if windows users are used.

3. SQL Server Instance – Database (could be SQL Express) where "LoadTest2010" DB would be placed and to be used as result repository.

4. "Apply Settings" once done

Agents

Demystifying Scalability

On identified Agent machine(s), "Visual Studio Test Agent Tool" is required to be installed. Once the installation is done, open "Configure test Agent", below screen would be loaded;

1. Username – It should be same as Controller (either domain user or Windows user)

2. Password – It should also be same as Controller user that is used for configuring load test controller.

3. Register with Test Controller – Specify Controller machine IP or Name with a port number as "6901". This port is used by Controller and Agents for their communication.

4. "Apply Setting" once done

Creating Load Test Project

Demystifying Scalability

Open VSTS (Ultimate) and navigate to create a new Project, below window will appear. Select "Web Performance and Load test Project", provide a path in "Location", name your project and solution and click "OK".

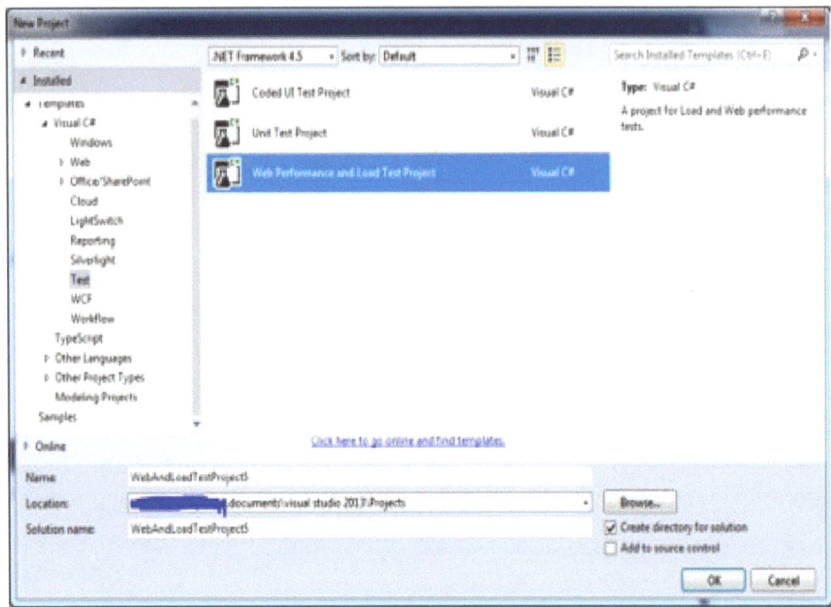

A Solution and project will get created with default files including "loadtestsettings" and a "webtest"

Load Test setting – It can be for remote (for Agents) or Local (when only controller is used to do a load test).

WebTest – it's a file that is actually a test script.

Demystifying Scalability

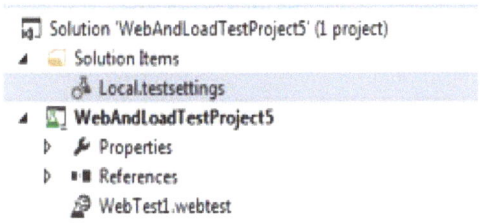

Record Web Test

Open a ".webtest" file and click on "Add recording". It will open a browser (by default – internet explorer).

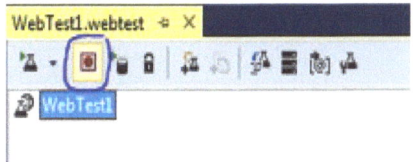

Put your application website address that you planned to test for and navigate your scenario. In this case for an example, I am putting bing search as an example; While navigating, Web test recorder will record all the calls as below. Note that, if "Web Test recorder" doesn't appear in your browser, you need to enable this add-on.

Demystifying Scalability

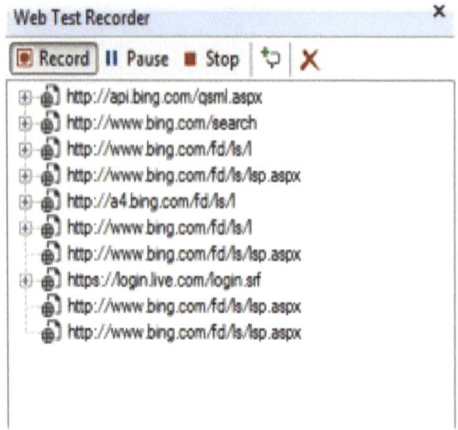

This will generate a web load test script with these same calls and parameterization that was used while navigating scenario;

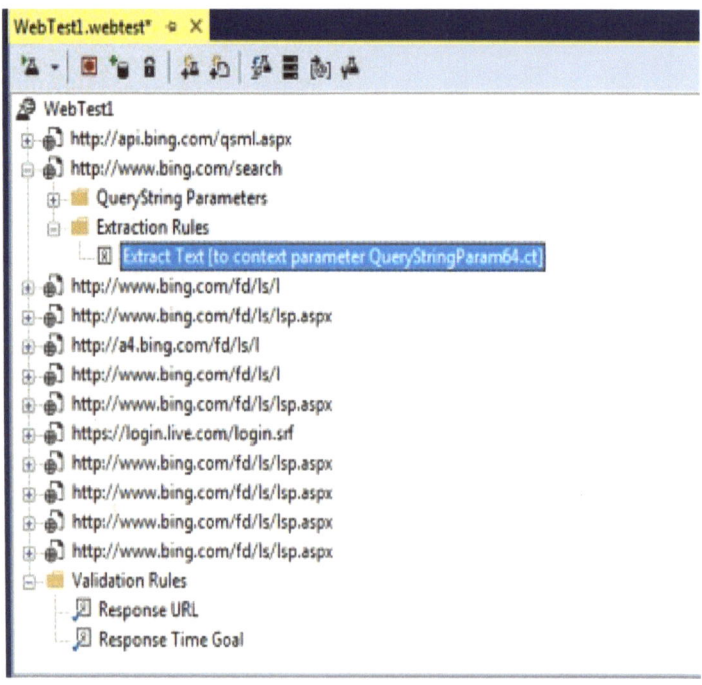

Demystifying Scalability

Parameterize your load test script using either .csv file, DB file or an XML.

Repeat above steps to create web test scripts for all identified scenarios. Once a web test scripts are ready, create a load test file for executing these script in a load test.

Load Test file creation

Right click on your project and click on "Add -> LoadTest". A load test file will be created. Open this file.

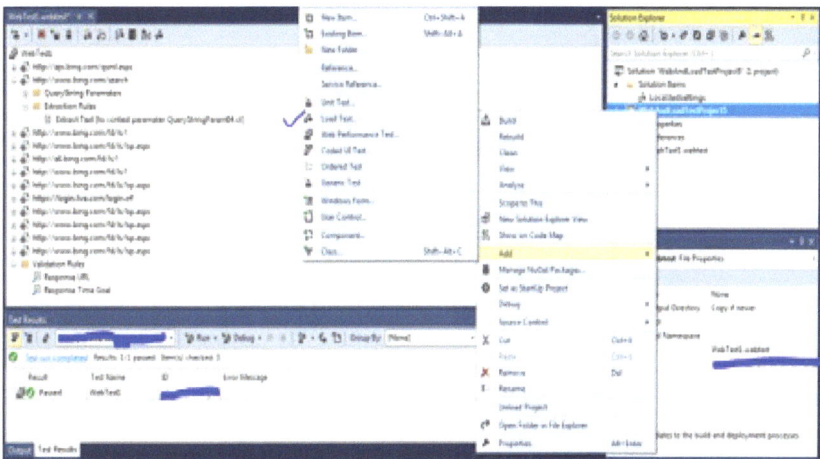

A Load test file creation wizard will open

Demystifying Scalability

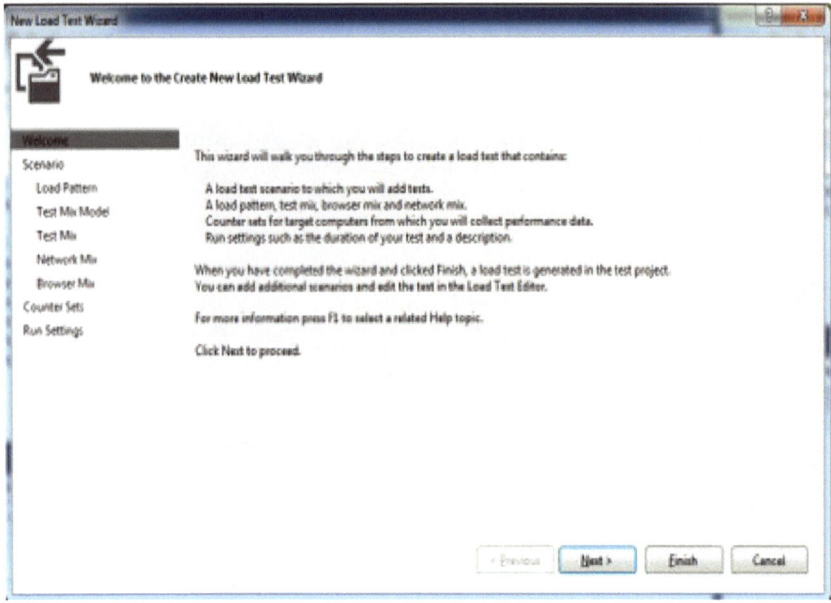

Click Next

Demystifying Scalability

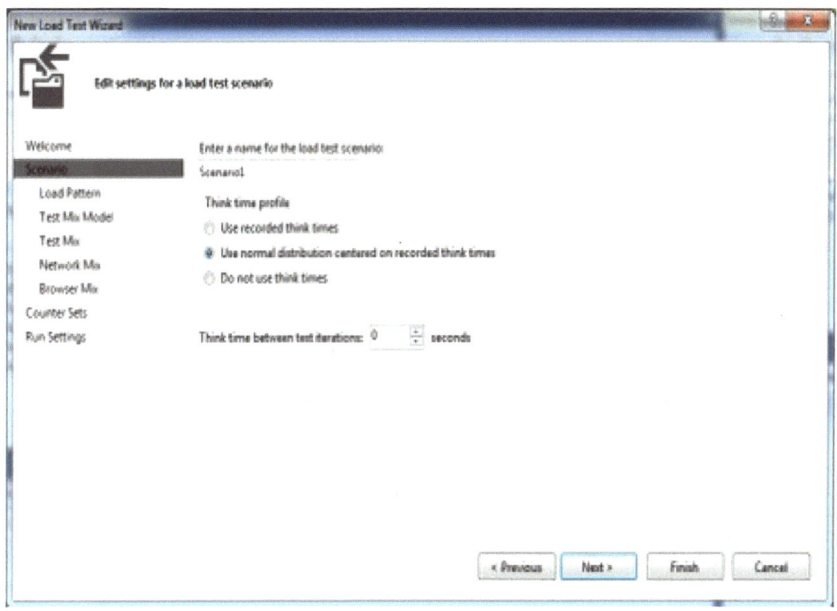

Scenario – Configuration about how you want to execute your web test scrtips.

"Use recorded think times" – It uses actual wait times that was spent on the screen while navigating a scenario.
"Use normal distribution centered on recorded think times" – VSTS will calculate think time values based on recorded time and use it during load test

"Do not use think times" – No wait time at all. All transactions will be executed without any delay.

"Think time between test iterations" – This is a time that a test will wait before starting next iteration of the test. It's a time between two test iterations.

Click "Next"

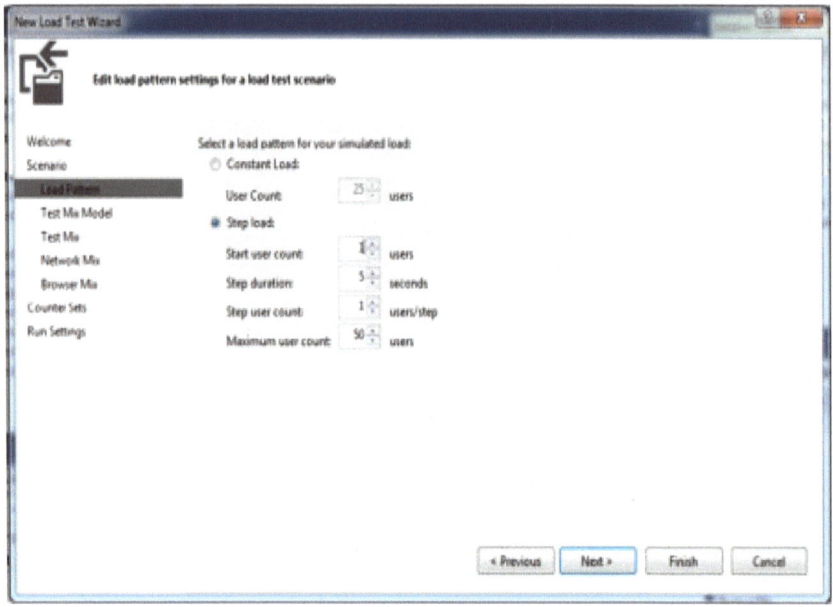

"Constant Load" – User load that will be constant from start throughout the test period

"Step Load" – User load will increase in steps starting with "Start user count". Load will increased in a step of "Step user count" every "step duration" sec till it reaches max user load mentioned in "Maximum user count". It will maintain max user load throughout the remaining test period.

It is always advisable to use step load.

Click "Next"

Demystifying Scalability

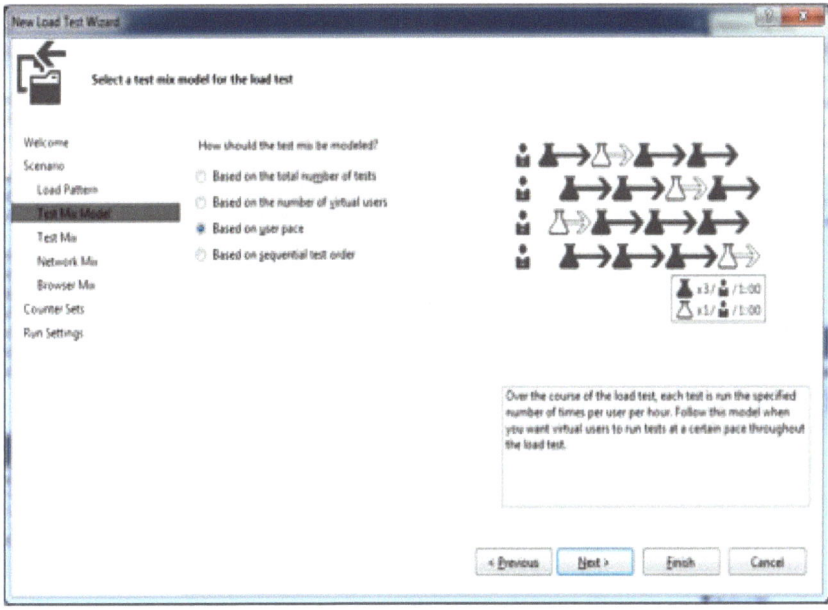

Select suitable text mix model. As I mentioned earlier, I prefer to use "Based on user pace" model, I will give example with this. Other test mix models can be learnt and experimented as well in the link I mentioned in "test approach" section.

Demystifying Scalability

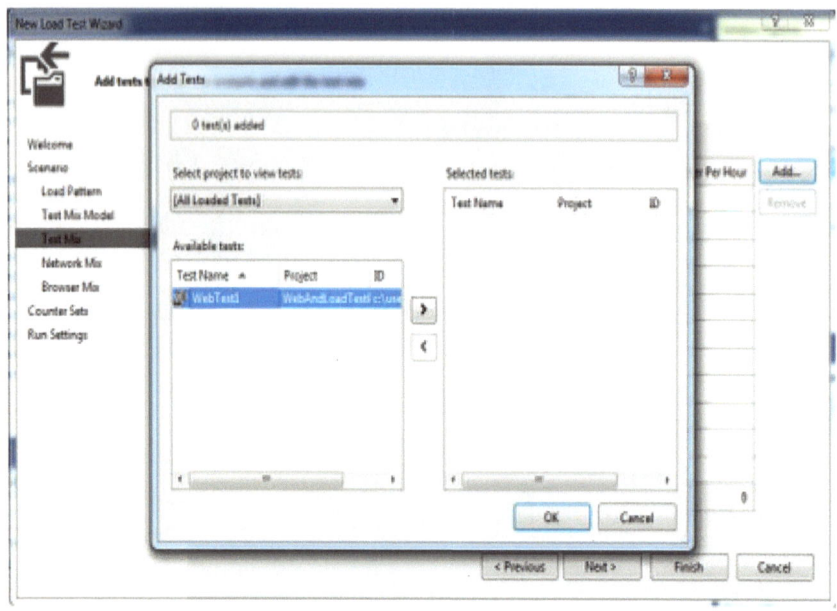

Test Mix window will appear on which click on Add on the prior window, "Add Tests" screen will appear. Here you have to add your web tests that you want to run in this load test file. Move selected tests to right and click OK, a test will be added in your test mix. You would need to specify throughput or iteration of the test executed by each user in an hour in "Test per user per hour" column;

Demystifying Scalability

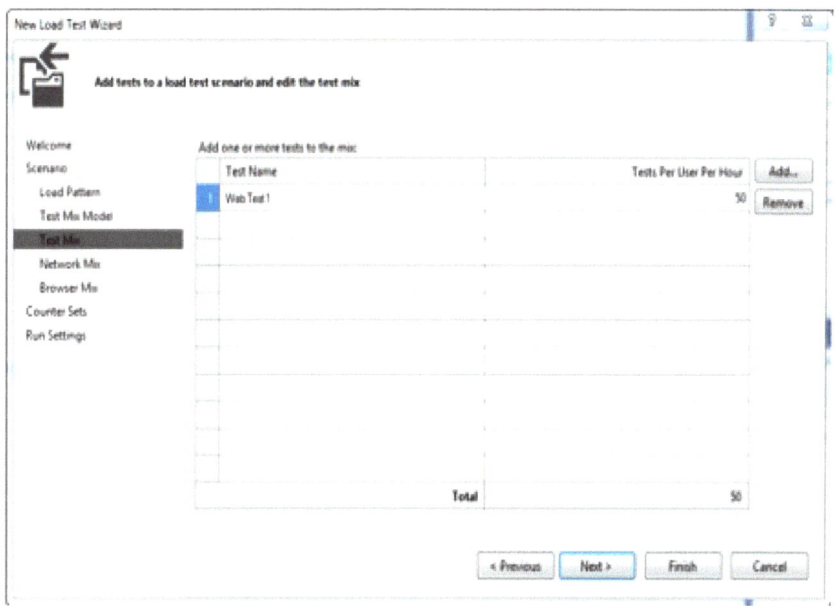

Click "Next"

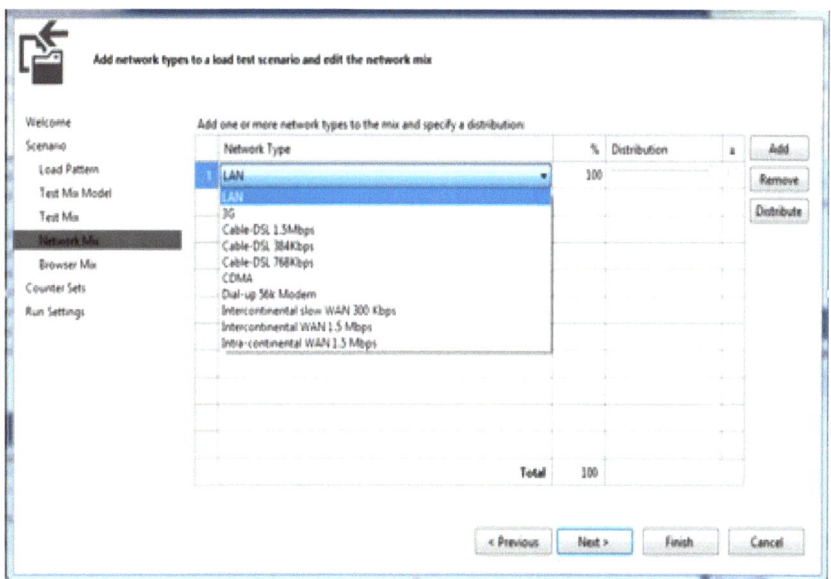

53

On this screen, you can select on which network you want to execute the test; LAN, Dial in, etc. Select appropriate network type and provide distribution of load you anticipate for each network type to simulate real life situations.

Click "Next"

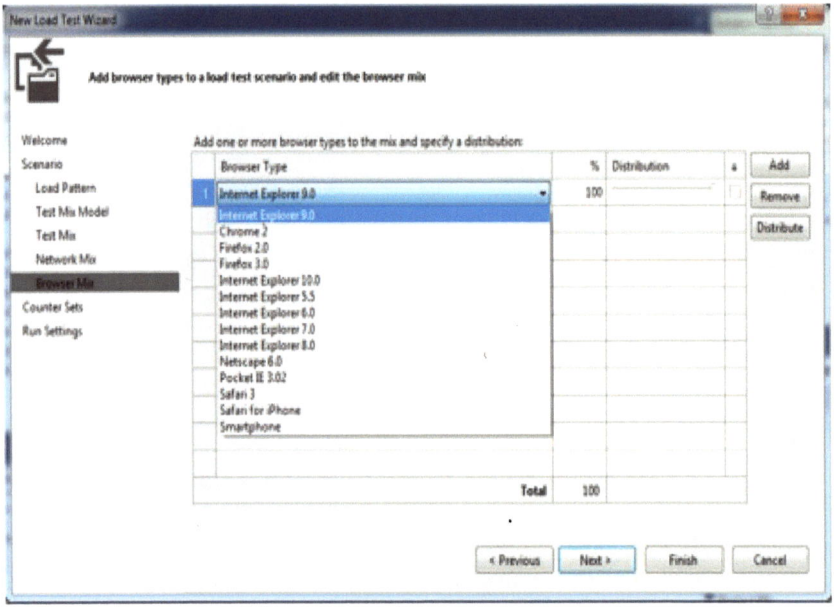

Similarly, in this step you can distribute the load for different browser type with respect to anticipated user load to simulate real life situations.

Click "Next"

Demystifying Scalability

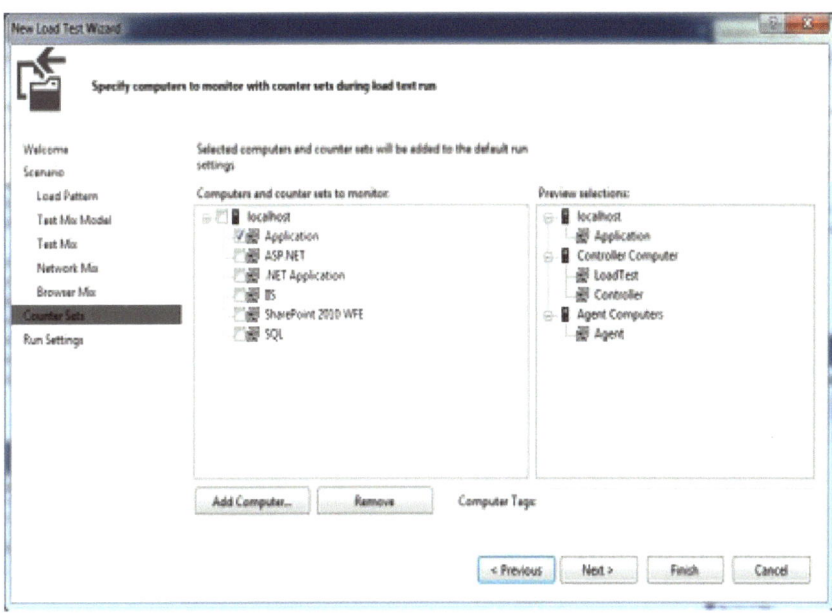

On this screen, you can add computers (machines) which are directly accessible from controller and has appropriate rights given to Controller use to capture performance counters. You can either capture counters through VSTS using this method or using "Perfmon" running on each web server which you will be hitting while executing the test manually. Select appropriate counter for machine you have added if you wish to use VSTS to capture those counters.

Benefit of using VSTS to capture counters are that VSTS will feed in this data to its loadTest2010 DB which it creates as a repository to save results.

Click "Next"

Demystifying Scalability

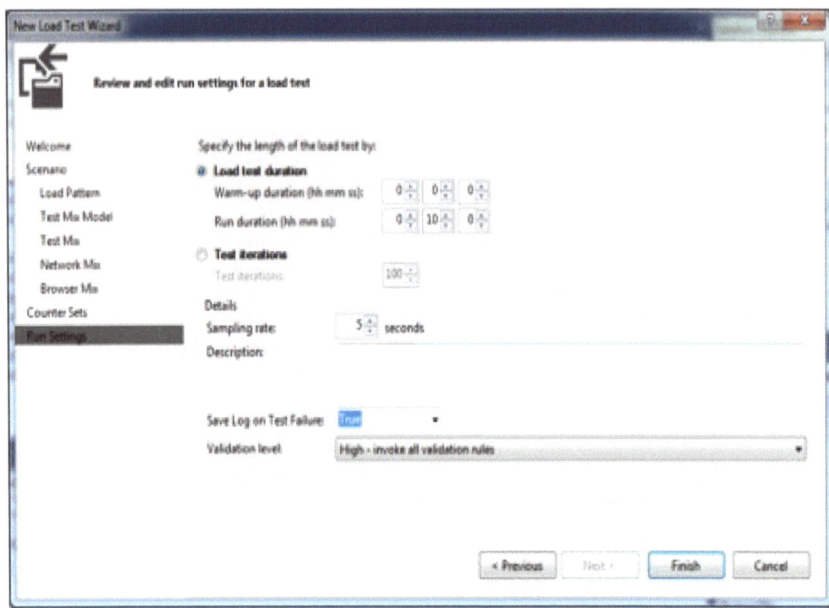

Finally you have to choose your run settings. Whether you want to run the test based on specified time or with definite interval. In my approach, I choose to run tests for specified time interval. I usually run the test for an hour for better simulation. For Endurance Test, where you have to execute tests for longer duration, you need to choose "Load test duration".

Test iteration option is like executing the tests for certain iterations that once it reaches, VSTS will end the test.

Sampling rate – it's the rate at which VSTS will capture its counter related to Controller, Agents, Machines specified and all the test details like page response time, scenario response time, user load, etc.

Click "Finish", it will create a ".loadtest" file.

Demystifying Scalability

Load Test execution

Since all the settings are done while configuring load test file, you can start executing load test by clicking "Run"

When you click "Run" bottom section should show;

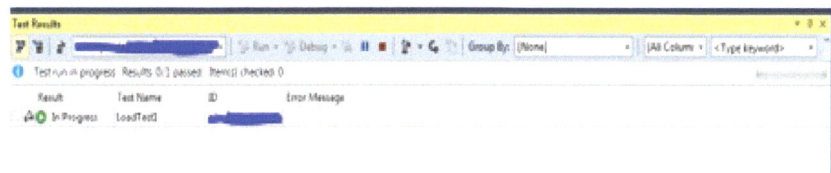

Test will start and below screen will appear;

Demystifying Scalability

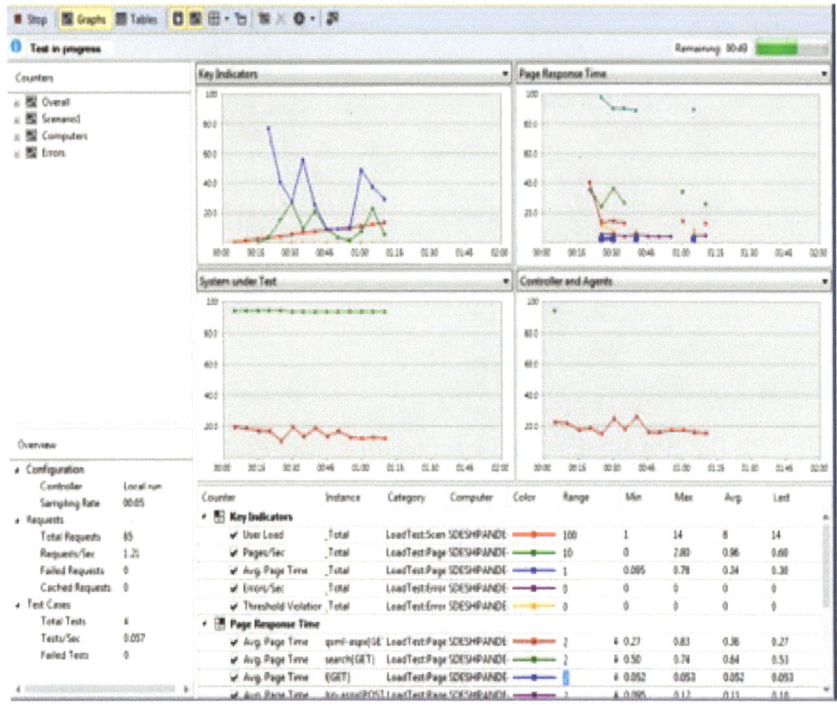

Key Indicator – Graphs of user load, pages per sec, Avg page time, Errors per sec and Threshold violations.

Page Response time – Graphs of response time of all the pages executed in the tests

System Under Test – Shows resource utilization of the machines added to capture performance counters.

Controller and Agents – Shows resource utilization of Controller and Agent machines.

Load Test Analysis

Once the test is completed, all these graphs will be full and Summary will be

Demystifying Scalability

displayed;

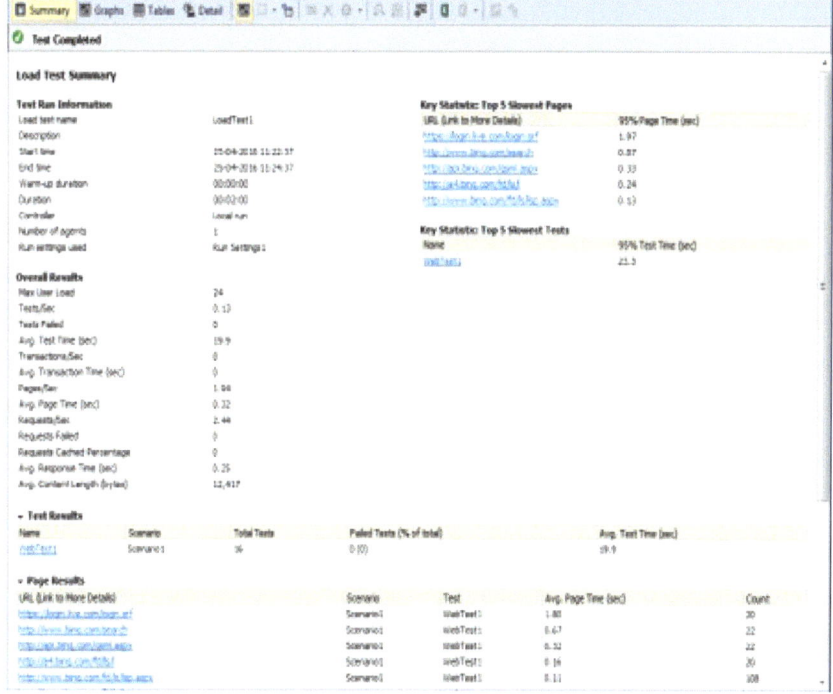

Click on "Graphs" to view graphs that was visible while execution was ON

Demystifying Scalability

Tables will show you numerical representation of your tests.

When you hover over mouse on any of the execution line, it will show you details of the test that got completed like which virtual user has executed the test, how much time it took and its test duration. Here you can see various statistics like Page Response Time, CPU, Memory change as number of concurrent users increase. You can record these numbers for a given version of software. If any of statistics are above SLA, then you can log a bug, have developer fix it and then repeat the test until numbers are within SLA.

Demystifying Scalability

Summary

Thank you for taking time to read this book. You are now well versed with Scalability, load testing and how to use VSTS to perform load testing. Scalability testing is critical skill to have in services world. Applying scalability testing to software application solves a lot of latency and throughput problems early in and result in creating highly performant apps for end users.

www.ingramcontent.com/pod-product-compliance
Lightning Source LLC
Chambersburg PA
CBHW040847180526
45159CB00001B/341